PRIMARY SOURCES OF
FAMOUS PEOPLE IN AMERICAN HISTORY™

JESSE JAMES

WESTERN BANK ROBBER

KATHLEEN COLLINS

rosen central
Primary Source™
The Rosen Publishing Group, Inc., New York

Published in 2004 by The Rosen Publishing Group, Inc.
29 East 21st Street, New York, NY 10010

Copyright © 2004 by The Rosen Publishing Group, Inc.

First Edition

Library of Congress Cataloging-in-Publication Data

Collins, Kathleen.
Jesse James : Western bank robber / Kathleen Collins.— 1st ed.
   v. cm. — (Famous people in American history)
Contents: Jesse James's early life — Jesse James and the James Gang — Wanted, dead or alive — The end of a famous outlaw — Making of a legend.
ISBN 0-8239-4112-4 (library binding)
ISBN 0-8239-4184-1 (pbk.)
6-pack ISBN 0-8239-4311-9
1. James, Jesse, 1847-1882—Juvenile literature. 2. Outlaws—West (U.S.)—Biography—Juvenile literature. 3. Frontier and pioneer life—West (U.S.)—Juvenile literature. 4. West (U.S.)—History—1860-1890—Juvenile literature. 5. West (U.S.)—Biography—Juvenile literature. [1. James, Jesse, 1847-1882. 2. Robbers and outlaws. 3. Frontier and pioneer life—West (U.S.) 4. West (U.S.)—History—1860-1890.] I. Title. II. Series.
F594.J27C65 2004
364.15'52'092—dc21

                                                              2003001996

Manufactured in the United States of America

Photo credits: cover © Hulton/Archive/Getty Images; p. 5 Library of Congress Prints and Photographs Division, HABS, MO, 11-SAJOE, 9-1; pp. 6, 22 Library of Congress Geography and Map Division; pp. 7, 14, 23, 27 Library of Congress Prints and Photographs Division; pp. 8 (X-22139), 9 (X-22154), 15 (X-21822) Denver Public Library, Western History Collection; p. 11 © Bettmann/Corbis; pp. 12, 13 Collection of David Carroll; pp. 16, 17 courtesy of Northfield Historical Society, Northfield, MN; p. 19 courtesy of Missouri State Archives; p. 21 courtesy of State Historical Society of Missouri, Columbia; p. 25 © Corbis; p. 26 © National Portrait Gallery, Smithsonian Institution/Art Resource, NY; p. 29 Center for Popular Music, MTSU.

Designer: Thomas Forget; Photo Researcher: Rebecca Anguin-Cohen

CONTENTS

1 JESSE JAMES'S EARLY LIFE

Jesse James was born in Missouri on September 5, 1847. His father, Robert, was a minister. Robert James was also a farmer. He died in 1851. In 1857, Jesse's mother, Zerelda, married a farmer and doctor named Reuben Samuels. Jesse and his older brother, Frank, were raised as farm boys.

DID YOU KNOW?

When they were young, the James brothers were good, honest boys. They worked hard on the farm. They went to church on Sundays, and they were well behaved. They were loyal to their family.

When Jesse James was growing up, he and his family lived at the corner of 12th Street and Michell Avenue in the town of St. Joseph, Missouri. This is a photo of their house.

When Jesse James was sixteen, the Civil War broke out. The Civil War, which started in 1861 and ended in 1865, was a very bloody battle. Sometimes friends would kill each other because they were on different sides. Jesse's parents were Confederates. Jesse and his brother were on the side of the South, too.

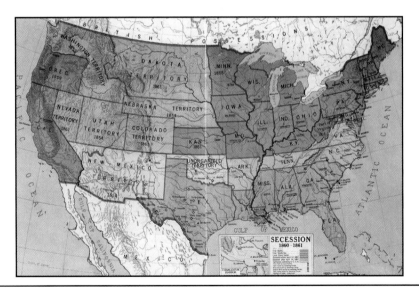

This wall map by Albert Bushnell Hart shows how the United States was divided during the Civil War. In this battle, the North was called the Union and the South was called the Confederacy.

This 1862 photo shows Union soldiers at a signal station on Elk Mountain in Maryland during the Battle of Antietam. At signal stations, soldiers put up flags that would let other soldiers know what their plans were.

During the Civil War, Jesse's family home was attacked by enemies from the North. This made Jesse angry. He decided to become an outlaw. In 1862, Jesse and Frank joined a band of Confederate rebels in Missouri and Kansas. They attacked farms and communities that were on the side of the North.

QUANTRILL'S RAIDERS

Frank and Jesse joined William Clarke Quantrill's gang, Quantrill's Raiders. Quantrill was born in 1837 in Ohio and died in 1865. Quantrill's gang terrorized many people. This is a photo of him.

Jesse James and his brother, Frank, posed for this portrait sometime between 1866 and 1876. The photo was taken at a photographer's studio, like the portrait of Quantrill on page 8.

2 JESSE JAMES AND THE JAMES GANG

In 1866, Jesse and Frank formed their own band of outlaws. A Confederate rebel named Cole Younger and his brothers joined the James brothers. They were known as the James Gang. There were about twelve members. Jesse was the gang leader. They committed robberies and killed people in several states, including Iowa, Alabama, and Texas.

DID YOU KNOW?

During the Civil War, Frank and Jesse also joined a band of outlaws led by a man named Bloody Bill Anderson. Bloody Bill had formed his own outlaw band in the spring of 1863. He was killed by federal troops in 1864. Quantrill's Raiders and Bloody Bill's Rebels made raids on antislavery towns and Union soldiers. They became well-known bandits.

Cole Younger was born in Jackson County, Missouri, in 1844. In 1876, Cole and two of his brothers, James and Robert, were captured after robbing a bank in Northfield, Minnesota.

On February 13, 1866, Jesse and Frank robbed a bank in Liberty, Missouri. They stole thousands of dollars and killed a bystander. Many people say it was the first bank robbery to take place during the day. The James Gang became famous all around the United States. Some people wrote stories and songs about them.

Jesse James *(right)* and Belle Star. There are only about 25 known photos of Jesse. Belle Star was not a member of his gang, but she helped them.

These never-before-published cabinet cards feature gang members Jim Younger *(top)* and his brother, Cole Younger *(bottom)*. In the late 1800s, cabinet cards were used as a sort of visiting card. Cabinet cards with portraits (such as these) became popular in 1866.

The James Gang continued to steal gold and money from stagecoaches, stores, banks, and people from Iowa to Alabama and Texas. On July 21, 1873, they robbed a train for the first time on the Rock Island Railroad in Adair, Iowa. They would continue their lives of crime for more than fifteen years.

The Rock Island Railroad was the first train that connected Chicago to the Mississippi River. This is a photo of Rock Island Engine No. 659 at Valley Junction, Iowa, in 1924.

In the 1800s, horse-drawn stagecoaches were used to take people to places where trains couldn't go. This photo shows women and girls on a stagecoach in Colorado. Many bandits, like Jesse James, held up stagecoaches and robbed the passengers.

3 WANTED: DEAD OR ALIVE

On September 7, 1876, the James Gang robbed a bank in Northfield, Minnesota. Many people were killed during the robbery. Three members of the gang were captured and put in jail for life. Only Jesse and Frank James escaped. After the robbery, the brothers hid in Nashville, Tennessee, for more than three years.

This is an early postcard image of the interior of the First National Bank (built in 1868), which the James Gang robbed. In 1975, the Northfield Historical Society in Minnesota bought the building. It is now a museum.

REWARD!

- DEAD OR ALIVE -

$5,000.$^{.00}_{x\ x}$ will be paid for the capture of the men who robbed the bank at

NORTHFIELD, MINN.

They are believed to be Jesse James and his Band, or the Youngers.

All officers are warned to use precaution in making arrest. These are the most desperate men in America.

Take no chances! Shoot to kill!!

J. H. McDonald,

SHERIFF

After the famous robbery of the Northfield bank in 1876, this "wanted" poster was put up to help capture the dangerous outlaws. A $5,000 reward was offered. Even today, police departments use "wanted" posters to help capture criminals.

In 1880, a lawyer named William H. Wallace wanted the outlaws to be arrested. Governor Thomas T. Crittenden of Missouri offered a $10,000 reward for the capture of the James brothers. He would pay the reward if the brothers were brought to him either dead or alive.

TOUGH JESSE JAMES

Jesse James was a very tough outlaw. He even killed one of his gang members because he thought the man was not being loyal to him.

Thursday July 28th 1881.

The Governor issued the following
Proclamation:
State of Missouri
Executive Department

Whereas it has been made known to me, as the governor of the State of Missouri, that certain parties, whose names are to me unknown, have confederated and banded themselves together for the purpose of committing robberies and other depredations within this state; and

Whereas said parties did on or about the eighth day of October 1879, stop a train near Glendale in the county of Jackson in said state, and with force and violence take, steal and carry away the money and other express matter being carried thereon, and

Whereas, on the 15th day of July, 1881, said parties and their confederates did stop a train upon the line of the Chicago Rock Island and Pacific Railway Company, near Winston in the county of Daviess in said state, and with force and violence take, steal and carry away the money and other express matter being carried thereon; and

Whereas, in perpetration of the robbery last aforesaid, the parties engaged therein did kill and murder one William Westfall the conductor of the train aforesaid, together with one John McCulloch who was at the time in the employ of said company then on said train; and

Whereas Frank James and Jesse W. James stand indicted in the circuit court of Daviess county in the state aforesaid for the murder of John W. Sheets; and

Whereas the parties engaged in the robberies and murders aforesaid, and each of them, have fled from justice and have absconded and secreted themselves:

Now Therefore in consideration of the premises, and in lieu of all other rewards heretofore offered for the arrest or conviction of the parties aforesaid or either of them by any person or corporation I, Thomas T. Crittenden, governor of the state

In this letter, Governor Crittenden offers a $10,000 reward for the capture of the James brothers. This was the largest reward that had ever been offered for a criminal in the United States.

4 THE END OF A FAMOUS OUTLAW

Jesse was living in St. Joseph, Missouri, with his wife and children. Jesse had married Zerelda Mimms on April 24, 1874. It may have seemed like he was living a quiet life with his family. But he was not finished with his outlaw life. He was pretending that his name was Thomas Howard so that he would not get caught.

MRS. JESSE JAMES

Zerelda Mimms was born July 21, 1845. She was engaged to Jesse for nine years before they were married on April 24, 1874. Zerelda was Jesse's first cousin. They had four children. A son, Jesse Edward, and a daughter, Mary Susan, survived. Their other two children died. Their names were Gould and Montgomery.

Zerelda Amanda Mimms is most famous for being the wife of Jesse James. She was one of twelve children of Mary (James) and John W. Zimms. Zerelda, or Zee as she was called, was born in Logan County, Kentucky.

A man named Robert Ford was a member of Jesse's gang. He wanted to try to get the reward money all for himself. He also wanted to be known as the person who killed the famous Jesse James. He went to Jesse's home in St. Joseph, Missouri, in the spring of 1882.

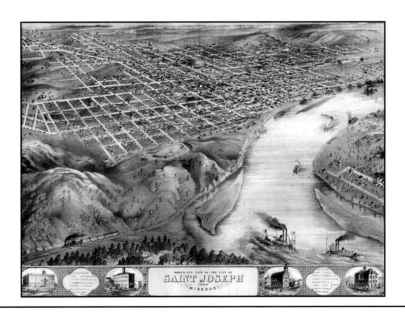

This 1868 lithograph shows the town of St. Joseph, where Jesse James was living when he was murdered. The town is situated on the Missouri River, close to the state line of Kansas.

Robert Newton Ford was just a teenager when he joined Jesse's gang as a bandit. He said he was Jesse's friend, but he had other plans. Ford told Governor Crittenden that he would capture Jesse James.

Jesse invited Robert Ford and his brother Charley into his home to plan another robbery in Missouri. Jesse trusted Ford. He even took off his guns and put them on a table. While Jesse turned his back, Ford shot Jesse and killed him. Jesse James died on April 3, 1882.

THE LEGEND LIVES ON

A lot of songs were made up about the death of Jesse James. This is a common one.

> *Jesse had a wife*
> *She's a mourner all her life,*
> *Her children they are brave;*
> *Oh! the dirty little coward*
> *who shot Mister Howard*
> *And laid Jesse in his grave.*
>
> *It was Robert Ford, that dirty little coward*
> *I wonder how he does feel,*
> *For he ate of Jesse's bread*
> *And he slept in Jesse's bed,*
> *Then he laid Jesse James in his grave.*

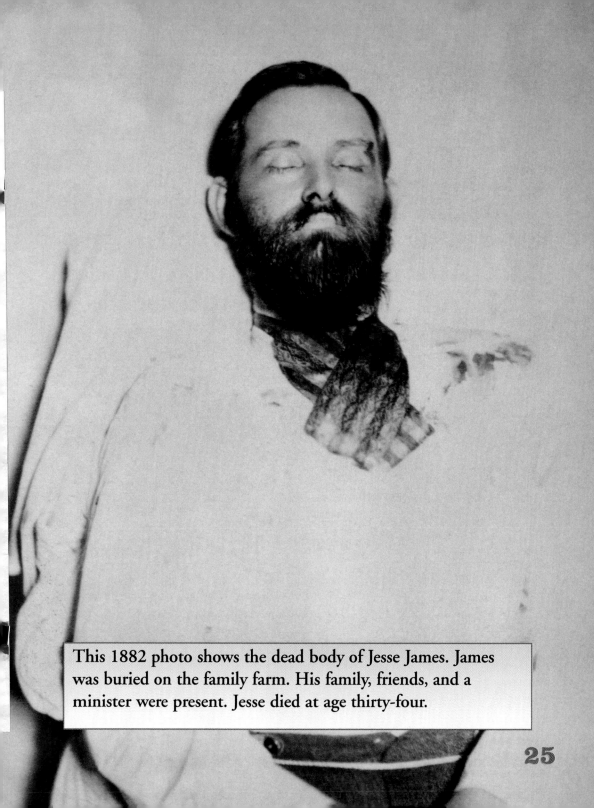

This 1882 photo shows the dead body of Jesse James. James was buried on the family farm. His family, friends, and a minister were present. Jesse died at age thirty-four.

5 MAKING OF A LEGEND

In the end, Robert Ford did not get the reward. Governor Crittenden had offered Ford a pardon if he killed Jesse. Ford was found guilty of murder, but the governor kept his promise and let him go free. Frank James gave himself up six months after his brother Jesse died.

This wood engraving of Jesse James was published in Frank Leslie's *Illustrated Newspaper* in 1882.

This grouping of photos, from 1882, shows some of the main elements in what became known as the legend of Jesse James: Jesse's dead body *(center)*, Mrs. Zerelda Samuels, Jesse's mother *(bottom left)*; the James farm *(bottom right)*; Robert Ford *(top right)*; and his brother, Charley *(top left)*.

Many legends and songs were written about Jesse James and the James Gang. Some people thought of them as heroes because people said they stole from the rich and gave to the poor. But Jesse most likely made up that myth himself. Today, Jesse and Frank James are among the best-known Americans in history.

LONG LIVE JESSE JAMES

This is another song that people sang about Jesse James long after his death.

> *Jesse James was one of his names,*
> *Another it was Howard.*
> *He robbed the rich of every stitch,*
> *You bet, he was no coward.*

JESSE JAMES

WORDS BY
ROGER LEWIS
MUSIC BY
F. HENRI KLICKMAN

5

WILL ROSSITER
THE CHICAGO PUBLISHER
136 W. LAKE ST. CHICAGO, ILL
ALBERT L. SON SYDNEY AUSTRALIA.
Copyright MCMXI by Will Rossiter

This 1911 song is about Robert Ford shooting Jesse James. Jesse James was so interesting that people kept on writing songs about him long after he was dead.

TIMELINE

1847—Jesse James is born in Missouri on September 5.

1851—Jesse's father dies.

1857—Jesse's mother, Zerelda, marries Dr. Reuben Samuels.

1861-1865— The Civil War.

1862—Frank and Jesse join William Quantrill's band of rebels.

1866—Jesse and Frank form the James Gang. They rob a bank in Liberty, Missouri, on February 13.

1873—The James Gang robs a train on the Rock Island Railroad.

1874—Jesse marries Zerelda Mimms on April 24.

1876—The James Gang robs a bank in Northfield, Minnesota.

1879—The James brothers form a new gang.

1880—Governor Crittenden offers a reward for the capture of the James brothers.

1882—Robert Ford kills Jesse James on April 3. Frank James gives himself up.

GLOSSARY

bystander (BY-STAND-er) Someone who is just watching something happen but is not part of the action.

capture (KAP-chur) To take a person by force.

Confederacy (kun-FEH-duh-reh-see) The eleven Southern states that declared themselves separate from the United States in 1860 and 1861.

guilty (GIL-tee) When someone has done something wrong.

lawyer (LOY-er) A person who gives advice about the law and who speaks for people in court.

loyal (LOY-uhl) Faithful to a person or an idea.

myth (MITH) A story that people make up to explain events.

outlaw (OWT-law) A criminal, especially one who is running away from the law.

pardon (PAR-duhn) To excuse someone who did something wrong.

rebel (REH-bul) A person who fought for the South during the Civil War.

reward (reh-WARD) Something you get in return for doing something good.

WEB SITES

Due to the changing nature of Internet links, the Rosen Publishing Group, Inc., has developed an online list of Web sites related to the subject of this book. This site is updated regularly. Please use this link to access the list:

http://www.rosenlinks.com/fpah/jjam

PRIMARY SOURCE IMAGE LIST

Page 5: Photo of Jesse James's house in St. Joseph, Buchanan County, Missouri. No date. Image from the Library of Congress.

Page 7: Photo of Union soldiers at signal station during Battle of Antietam. Photo taken October 1862. Image from Library of Congress.

Page 8: Photo of William Clarke Quantrill, dated between 1860 and 1865. Image housed at Denver Public Library.

Page 9: Photo of Jesse and Frank James, dated between 1866 and 1876. Image from the Denver Public Library.

Page 11: Photo of Cole Younger, dated 1976. The photo is from Bettman Archives.

Page 12: Cabinet cards of Jesse James and Belle Star. Approximate date, 1866. Collection of David Carroll.

Page 13: Cabinet card of Tim Younger. Approximate date, 1902. Cabinet card of Cole Younger dated between 1903 and 1916. Collection of David Carroll.

Page 14: Photo of Rock Island Engine No. 659 at Valley Junction, Iowa. Image from Library of Congress.
Page 15: Photo of stagecoach in Colorado, dated between 1905 and 1915. Image from the Denver Public Library.
Page 17: Reward poster from Northfield Historical Society, dated 1876.
Page 19: Letter from Missouri governor Thomas T. Crittenden, dated Thursday, July 28, 1881. From Missouri State Archives.
Page 21: Woodcut of Zerelda Mimms, no date. Image from the State Historical Society of Missouri.
Page 23: Photo of Robert Ford, dated 1889. From the Library of Congress.
Page 25: Photo of body of Jesse James, 1882, taken by a photographer named R. Uhlman.
Page 27: Montage of photos: Jesse James's corpse, Zerelda Samuels, the James Farm, Robert Ford and his brother, Charley Ford. Photo taken 1882. Images from the Library of Congress.

INDEX

ABOUT THE AUTHOR

Kathleen Collins was born in Rochester, New York. She is a writer and researcher who now lives in New York City. She loves to learn and write about American history.